A Life REdone

A Life REdone

My **Journey** to a **Life** of **Freedom**

Laura Eve Harding

authorHOUSE®

AuthorHouse™
1663 Liberty Drive
Bloomington, IN 47403
www.authorhouse.com
Phone: 1 (800) 839-8640

All Scripture quotations, unless otherwise indicated, are taken from The Holy Bible. King James Version (KJV). Outside of the United Kingdom, the KJV is in the public domain. Within the United Kingdom, the rights to the KJV are vested in the Crown. This Bible is printed and published by Cambridge University Press, the Queen's royal printer, under royal letters patent. The text commonly available now is actually that of the 1769 revision, not that of 1611. The text used by BLB is the current 1769 edition. Other Scripture references are from the following sources: New King James Version (NKJV). Copyright © 1982 by Thomas Nelson, Inc. All rights reserved. Used by permission. New International Version (NIV). Copyright © 1973, 1978, 1984, 2011 by Biblica, Inc.® Used by Permission of Biblica, Inc.® All rights reserved worldwide. The Holy Bible. New Living Translation (NLT). Scripture quotations are taken from the Holy Bible, New Living Translation, copyright © 1996, 2004, 2007. Used by permission of Tyndale House Publishers Inc., Carol Stream, Illinois 60188. All rights reserved.

Published by AuthorHouse   05/13/2018

ISBN: 978-1-4918-1518-2 (sc)
ISBN: 978-1-4918-1519-9 (e)

Library of Congress Control Number: 2013916433

Print information available on the last page.

Any people depicted in stock imagery provided by Thinkstock are models, and such images are being used for illustrative purposes only.
Certain stock imagery © Thinkstock.

This book is printed on acid-free paper.

This book is dedicated to all young people in the world who feel there is no hope for their future. I was reminded and encouraged by a young woman in a school I work at that I should write this book. So for the encouragement to finish this book I would like to thank Alex B. I sure hope God can use my story as a stepping stone to encourage anyone struggling to find hope in their future to run in the right direction. Run toward the only One who can fill your aching hearts and ease your minds with His peace.

I would also like to thank all those that have encouraged me to finish this book, by giving their input and help. This includes Angela Alaniz, Laura Alexander, Charra Ewald, Tonia Harrison, Ms. Ballew, and many others. I would like to thank my mom Sherry Adolph, and my sister Sarah Coombs, Shannon Griffen and Mike LaFave too for their help with the details of the story. I would also like to thank my husband for his support in finishing this task! Most of all I would like to thank God for allowing me the privilege of writing this book to encourage those who so desperately need to find hope in the midst of uncertainty.

Contents

Introduction

    I am a woman who is passionate about my beliefs. Some years ago my life was changed forever. While traveling down my own path of winding roads, God stopped me from spiraling out of control, and lit up my world by meeting me right where I was. He showed me that I was alone, blind and helpless. He took a hold of me and shook up my world. I have not been the same since.

    The purpose of this book is to show my reader that they can have the same experience by coming to God in every situation. This book has been a project in the making for over five years, and I hope it does what I intended. Most importantly that it will accomplish what God has decided. He is ready and waiting for you to reach out to Him. Remember a masterpiece takes time to build (Ephesians 2:10).

The Truth
About Time

The grass withers and the flowers fade,
but the word of our God stands forever

(Isaiah 40:8, NLT).

If you're anything like me, you may spend some weeks just counting down the days until Friday, because relief comes on Friday. So starting on Monday, you watch the clock, even as you are consumed with your work or studies, counting down the days, the hours and finally the minutes until Friday hits. Before you know it, the weekend is gone, even if you did nothing productive or enjoyable to pass the time, and it is Monday again. Back to work or school you go.

That is a lot like my story. Rush, rush, rush through life trying to get somewhere but never reaching for anything important. This also helps me to reflect on how fast time flies. As a person gets older, they feel the truth of that statement much more than in their adolescent years. Even if nothing exciting is happening in the present there is so much to look forward to in the future.

So often I see teenagers today waste their time, spinning their wheels, trying to figure out what this life is all about, but in their search they never really come to a full understanding. It's true to say that some life lessons can be learned from the insight of others and don't necessarily call for a tough battle, learning the hard way. In my case, understanding this concept didn't come until my adult years.

Why, you do not even know what will happen tomorrow. What is your life? You are a mist that appears for a little while and then vanishes
(James 4:14, NIV).

No matter your age or sex, no matter your social standing, there is one thing in life that is the same for all people; time. Time keeps moving and it stops for no one. It doesn't consider whether or not you're ready for the next season in your life. The clock ticks and no one can stop it. As time moves on, you must leave the past behind and move forward to grow and learn from your mistakes.

If there is one thing I can tell you to set the scene for the story you are about to read, it is that freedom comes with a price. Don't be misled. Freedom can be great if used wisely. On the other hand, it can be costly if mismanaged.

My life story didn't start like most other peoples.' It is not a story filled with many good memories, and that may be my fault. My life did not begin with right choices and rewards, rather it was filled with poor choices and heartache. I was a belligerent child who started fighting in a tough match that could not be won—not by me, anyhow. I was caught in a tug-of-war between good and evil, just to get knocked down and end up starting life all over again. I failed horribly, falling face first onto the ground, and it was only by the grace of God I got up, He wiped me off, and I found relief in the arms of my Savior, Jesus Christ.

The whole human race is fighting an unseen war. The battles each of us struggle against change from season to season in our lives. The battles I fight today might not be the same ones I fought 13 years ago, but they continue to come at me and launch me into spiritual valleys. In whatever shape my struggles may come, they usually beat me down and remind me that I can do nothing on my own (John 15:5). How I view whatever trial I'm facing is vital because this is when I can gain insight and perspective and grow the most. Nevertheless, I enjoy the mountaintop experiences when the Holy Spirit sweeps refreshing breezes into my life to keep me going. In a period of seventeen years, I experienced the good, the bad and the ugly—enough for two lifetimes—but regardless, I can say that I've been blessed beyond what anyone can hope.

Thinking question:

What is it that you expect to get out of this book?

I suggest writing your thoughts down while reading and see what truths come to light that you know need to be addressed in your own life. As I am putting myself out there to share my failures with you, I hope that you are made aware of the things that lurk deep within your own self.

_____

_____

_____

_____

_____

_____

_____

_____

_____

_____

_____

_____

_____

_____

_____

_____

_____

_____

The Beginning

But those who trust in the LORD will find new
strength. They will soar high on wings like eagles.
They will run and not grow weary.
They will walk and not faint

(Isaiah 40:31, NLT).

Whenever a life-story or testimony is shared by someone it usually begins with a glimpse back into a person's best and worst memories from childhood. For me, the bad memories outweigh any good ones. As I reminisce, these memories are comprised of three people; my mom, my dad and my sister.

When my parents got married my mom was 26 and my dad was 31. Before they were married my mom had already given birth to me. Two-and-a-half years later my sister came into this world. Around that time my dad was given custody of his two young sons from a previous marriage. Some time after that, my dad handed over the responsibility of discipline to my mom. He gave her his leather belt and told to her to use it if anyone stepped out of line.

Six of us were stuffed into tight living quarters. My parents worked hard to take care of our family, but money was tight. My dad worked in the family advertising agency for a period of time, but after they had to downsize he lost his job. He started working the weekends at the Christian TV station while delivering newspapers on the night shift. For a short time, he even took the position as music director at our church. He loved truckers and felt called to minister Jesus to them when given the opportunity to do so. In the mix of his daily life my dad wasn't getting the right amount of sleep he needed to keep himself healthy because he had epilepsy.

From my perspective my dad was an amazing person. Even now, others who knew my father would say that he was a warm person who was tender to the very core. He wasn't always that way, but during the last ten years of his life God changed his heart and he became a softy. My dad had integrity, which meant that he was a man of his word. He was a gentle person who genuinely loved his family. He also had a great sense of humor. As a child I was drawn to my father much more than I was to my mother. It could have been for the reason that he was a light-hearted, silly guy. Or that I was a lot like my mom. Whatever the case, I loved my dad. I look like my dad and I am glad for that. My dad was unusual guy with an enormously big heart who I got to enjoy for just a few short years unfortunately.

Young as I was I do remember my family living in a constant state of chaos. I remember watching my father have seizures. One minute my dad would be standing up and then suddenly he would be laying flat on the ground with his body tossing from side to side, his eyes rolling around in his head. It was a frightening experience for a small child to witness. It is something that could never be erased from my memory. Unfortunately, my dad didn't like taking his medication regularly and he paid dearly for that. I think he would've rather felt normal, even during his worst days, than to have had to deal with being drugged up on seizure medication that made him feel like his head was in the clouds and I don't blame him.

When I was five years old my dad experienced a seizure in his sleep. Unfortunately, he'd had eaten a bowl of cereal before lying down to take a nap. The seizure was so intense he spit the food back up in his throat and choked on it. He was without air for more than five minutes and as a result he went into a coma from which he never awoke. Because of the amount of time he went without air, he would've been brain dead had he lived. He was just a few days short of his thirty-sixth birthday.

When my dad died my mom took over three or four paper routes that he'd done. Suddenly all the responsibility of taking care of our family fell on her and that's a heavy load for anyone to bear. Not too long after my dad passed away my brothers moved back to their mom's house. That left my mom, my sister and me. I remember on the weekends and the holidays my mom would stuff my sister and me into the back seat of the car wrapped in blankets, and we slept while she delivered newspapers in the early morning hours. People said she should've left us at home in our beds but she wouldn't do that. During the summer months my sister and I would help my mom with the paper routes in the afternoon. She'd drop us off with a hand-full of newspapers to deliver on the same street that she was working on. I remember some of her customers were gracious and caring. Occasionally they would leave us little treats to find on their porches.

The amount of time my dad was given on this earth was unfair; four days short of thirty-six years. I wonder to this day who even invented the word "fair?" What exactly is fair or even unfair and how and why is it relative to each individual? There certainly is no such thing as living a fair life here on earth with or without God. Nevertheless this isn't the end for those who know Him personally. We are just passing through on this earth and one day we will be united with God and other believers, both family and friends. The current limitations we face in mind, body and spirit will one day be perfected (Philippians 3:21).

Looking back now, the years following my dad's departure are scattered memories. However, I do recall many painful years that followed in which my mom, who was very young herself, raised my sister and me while working part-time and finishing college, all by the grace of God.

Thinking Question:

Can you think of any similar memories from when you were young that stand out as being unfair? If so write those down.

_____

_____

_____

_____

_____

_____

_____

_____

_____

_____

_____

_____

_____

_____

_____

_____

_____

_____

_____

_____

_____

The Trap

There is more hope for a fool than for someone who speaks without thinking

(Proverbs 29:20, NLT).

From the earliest time of my life I can remember feeling that my mom favored my younger sister, since I was always the one in trouble. My mom says that from the outside people would say that it looked as if she was two completely different people when it came to raising my sister and me. Truly I believe that my sister watched me do stupid things and get into trouble for them, and she was wise enough to learn from me. She was also a pretty obedient child and because of that I envied her with a passion. Over many years I referred to her as a "suck up." However true that was, it still was hard for me to understand. I don't remember feeling loved by my mom and I don't say that to hurt her, but that was how I saw it. (Although for my own reasons, on certain occasions I did manipulate my sister by taking her side of an issue when we were both on the hot seat. There were other times I'd pin her down to the floor and threatened to beat her up if she ratted me out for whatever I'd done.)

My mom had good intentions when raising me, she just didn't know how to teach me using the right means. Without showing love and grace while disciplining me as a child, I didn't understand it was for my own good that my mom was trying to teach me right from wrong. Little did I know that this would've been good for me to get down for use later in my life when I had to choose to submit to my bosses at work or lose my job. This was a tough lesson I should've learned in my early years but I resisted.

Even though I was a strong-willed child who didn't endure my mom's discipline without difficulty, I did have some good traits about me. They were often overlooked so I never learned how to utilize them in a productive manner. For example, I was always extremely stubborn and that could've been a strength, had I learned to use it in a positive manner. It could've kept me out of a lot trouble when it came to my peers pressuring me to do things that I shouldn't. As I've already said, I had a difficult time submitting to my mom as an authority figure because I didn't understand there was much more for me to learn from her that would help me in my future. Nevertheless, I allowed my stubbornness to be a stumbling block for me to continuously trip over. It made me fight yielding to authority, because I thought I knew what was best for me but what I really didn't understand was that I had a lot to learn.

My mom disciplined me the best she knew how, unsuccessfully using the "Spare the rod and spoil the child" method. When I was growing up my dad's leather belt hung on the back of her door. She spent many years chasing me around the house beating me with it. Sometimes when she couldn't a hold of the belt fast enough she'd wallop me with a wooden spoon or a spatula. There were also times that she'd grab onto me by the hair and throw my body around to position me for a beating. Over the years, I developed a set of lungs that could blow out someone's windows when I screamed. There were a few instances that the police came out to visit our house after they'd received a call about child abuse. My mom denied that she was ruthless and just kept on with her wicked temper. I don't think my mom realized then, during her fits of rage, just what she was doing or how out of control she was or even that these memories would be singed into my mind forever. These recollections caused me to become bitter and an intense hatred grew within me for my mom. I actually fought back as I got older and attempted to hit her and later on my step dad either with my fist or even by chucking an object at one of them.

It wasn't until I wrote this book that my mom shared with me specifically about how she was brought up. I've heard bits and pieces of how dysfunctional her family was but I really had no idea until recently. The vicious cycle of dysfunction that she was brought up in followed her right into our family. When she was young her mom and dad's relationship was a horrible one. Her mom had an obnoxious and critical attitude, and often times she pushed her husband to the extreme as she egged him on. When she was "stirring the pot," her dad's wicked temper would send him on a rampage and he became physically abusive to both my mom and her brother. She remembers an instance when her dad came after her with a baseball bat. Often while she was growing up, her mom would pack up and take off for months at a time and go back to her homeland in England. Her dad was a good father during those times. He picked up the slack for their mom. It was a much calmer atmosphere in their home when her mother wasn't around.

My grandfather also died young, while my mom was in her teens. Within a year her mother got remarried and offered to let my mom stay in the basement. She did for a short time and then moved out. Ultimately the validation she longed for from her family that she didn't get sent her searching elsewhere. Those bad habits my mom learned from her dad she brought into our family.

As I was growing up I continued to make bad choices habitually. I always got caught for doing wrong, and when I did I was severely punished. The worst part was that I never learned from my mistakes. For instance, I was a terrible liar. I couldn't honestly admit to a failure, even after I'd been caught in the act. For instance, my mom might've asked me if I'd done what she told me to and cleaned my closet out. Immediately, without thinking I would have blurted out yes. Then she'd go in my room and look in my closet and clearly see that I didn't, so I would get into trouble for lying and be stuck with the consequences. I'd even lie about something as stupid and obvious to anyone who was around me. For instance, after school on the way home from the bus stop I smoked a cigarette but when questioned at home about the stench that followed me, I'd lie and say I hadn't smoked. Or I'd lie and say that I had no homework but really I almost never brought it home to do. Almost everything that came out of my mouth was a lie, and because I didn't think before I spoke I was in trouble constantly. Not only did I lie to my family but I also lied to my friends on a pretty regular basis.

I can remember asking a friend many times if I could borrow money for lunch. Now I'd packed a cold lunch for myself every day but some days I didn't want it. I wanted hot lunch. What I really wanted was a bean burrito from Taco Bell in the school cafeteria. She would lend me the money to buy the burrito but I never paid her back even though I'd promised to. I was dishonest in my work responsibilities as well. I stole food and in some instances I stole money from the cash register. I lied to myself, blaming everyone else for my failures.

As I got older my mom changed her method of disciplining from beating me to grounding me. I was a very mouthy kid who didn't think before I spoke and often times I dug myself into a hole that I couldn't get out of. I can remember many times when my mom would be counting on her fingers how many weeks I was grounded for, while I spouted off disrespectful words at her. She would continue to count until I stopped. I'd always had to serve out my sentence completely too, no matter how many weeks she got up to. I spent much of my preteen and teenage years grounded in my room with absolutely no privileges, doing chores around the house, both inside and out, a technique my mom referred to as "work therapy." There are two instances that stand out in my mind of her using this technique to discipline me. One punishment I was given a few times was to wash the windows in the entire house, inside and out. When I didn't do a good job I'd have to go back and redo them. It's amazing as many times as I had that chore as a punishment I never got good at washing windows. To this day I hate washing windows. I can recall another time when my mom and step-dad had a cord of wood delivered to their house for bonfires. When delivered, it was put into a pile that measured four feet high, four feet wide, and eight feet long and it was dropped at the end of our driveway. There were at least two separate times that I had to move that entire pile from one side of the driveway to the other. It was a good punishment because aside from the labor it wasn't physically painful like a beating. It was also a kind of therapy that helped me to let off some steam as I worked off the anger that boiled inside of me. However annoying these punishments were they were still unsuccessful in teaching me. I was resistant to learning from them and so whatever offense I'd committed I'm sure I repeated over again.

Growing up without my dad was a living nightmare. Since the connection I had with my dad was strong and because the relationship with my mom was non-existent, I butted heads with her frequently. At home I felt like I had no allies or anyone who truly cared for me. As I endured consequences for my actions over and over again, my mind hardened and my heart grew cold and bitter. Emotions arose that cultivated within me a negativity that was strong enough to impact my life tremendously. Essentially, I blamed my mom for the death of my father. Consequently, I remained in bondage to Satan with my anger. Routinely as I dug myself deeper into much deceit, the fire that raged within me grew more intense, hardening my heart. This held me captive.

Of course, I had justification for my unresolved anger. My bad temper and lack of self-control was a huge problem for me. Instead of resolving to deal with these issues I just shoved them under the rug and denied I had them. The death of my dad and the harsh punishment I endured throughout my childhood was something I used as an excuse for my bad behavior. Now common sense should have alerted me to the fact that my emotions had no positive affect on me, but unfortunately, that light never came on, neither in my head nor in my heart. Even after growing up in church, and accepting Jesus as my Savior at the age of seven, I'd learned nothing that was tangible enough for me to have applied to my life that would've inspired me to be a person of integrity and most importantly to have surrendered myself to God.

A life filled with hate and self-loathing was what I'd accomplished and it took me nowhere. Essentially, I was caged in a life of self-pity. I was impetuous in my speech and actions, burdened with a heavy load of anger. I was disrespectful to any authority figure that didn't agree with me, especially my mom and later on my step-father.

There were at least a handful of times that my mom took me to my grandparents to have them pray something called a "warfare prayer" over me. It was like I had an evil spirit that resided within me that I couldn't get rid of and the prayer was supposed to cast that spirit out of me. I do remember feeling the oppression lift from me after that prayer but it would soon return because I wasn't schooled in how to fight these battles. I do however recall at least a couple of times going to conferences with my mom teaching about spiritual warfare but I never took the useful knowledge I could've gained. I think my mom and I could've benefited greatly if we took time to understand more about this. The battle that we fought with each other wasn't actually between her and me. It was something that Satan used to destroy our relationship and kept us pinned down in defeat.

Thinking Question:

Is there anything in your life, any issue, that you trip over and is coming to your mind as you read that needs to be weeded from your life?

_____

_____

_____

_____

_____

_____

_____

_____

_____

_____

_____

_____

_____

_____

_____

_____

_____

_____

_____

_____

_____

_____

_____

The Fall

We put our hope in the LORD.
He is our help and our shield

(Psalms 33:20, NLT).

As the years passed, the home in which my mom, sister and myself lived, was filled with too much animosity for a person to bear. I can't remember too many *good days* but instead many *stormy days* filled with issues. There were times when my mom and I went back and forth verbally assaulting each other. I had no idea what it meant to respect my mom, how to be obedient or to do what I was told with no questions asked. There were days I made choices and said things that I knew would come back to bite me but I didn't care. There were never times in my life that I spent considering the cost of my words and actions, good or bad. It was about the instant gratification of always "getting in the last word," or that is airing my opinion without restraint and not filtering what was coming out of my mouth. I did this with the hopes of leaving a conversation without a response, or at least a bad one from any authority figure. Thanks to my hindsight, I realize now that wasn't a good habit for me to have started because later on it was an extremely hard habit to quit.

My mother eventually decided delivering newspapers was not what she wanted to spend her life doing, so she went to college and earned a degree in accounting. She was 34 when she graduated. This was a giant step for my mom, as she was a high school drop-out who later got her GED. A college education and the jobs that resulted from it gave my mom the experience she needed to find a job that was good, but far from where we lived. I remember my mom coming home from work one day and announcing that we were moving away from our small-town life in mid-Michigan to a new city that was an hour and a half south of us. I was 12 when we relocated from our small town lifestyle to a larger city. I can remember being scared and excited all at the same time. My sister and I were leaving the only home we'd ever known. With all its unfamiliarity, it was scary step to take but we needed a fresh start to move on as a family. After spending many years saddened by the loss of my father, my mother decided this was the best thing for us; to move out and move on. We sold our house, packed up and moved south.

Prior to this, my mom had gone to singles dances and dated a bit. At one of the last dances she went to she met Keith. They dated for a year and then talked about getting married. It was not Keith's first marriage either. He had been married once before and this would be my mom's third marriage. God used my mom to introduce Keith to the Lord before they got married. Before we moved we started looking for a new church to join. My dad's family had close ties with the Southern Baptist church and they helped us locate another church of the same denomination near our new home.

Moving was a fresh start to make myself into whatever I wanted to be. Growing up in a small town was difficult because everyone knows every else's business. Because of the conditions my family resided in, underprivileged and poor, the kids at school picked on me. Not to mention the fact that I was a chubby tomboy. I just couldn't fit in with my peers. A new city, a new school, a new life, and things just might be different, or at least that is what I'd hoped.

It didn't take long for me to not only get back into my old habits but also to create new ones that were actually even more self-destructive. When we moved our city changed, our house changed, my school changed, but I was still the same person on the inside even though the circumstances around me had changed. The effects of my mom getting remarried were nothing but justification for my bad behavior, or at least it was that way in my mind. Once my mom and Keith got married, he took a stab at trying to make peace between my mom and me. Over the next few years Keith tried his best to stay out of the disciplining but when he periodically took the reins he became overbearing. He was strict and quite frankly a control freak, and that did not go over well with my sister and me.

In my new sphere I had a difficult time making friends, or at least friends of good influence. As long as I can remember, I gravitated toward the outsiders because that was how I'd felt as I was growing up. Unfortunately, following this pattern never led me where I needed to be. While I was growing up, I was constantly being compared to my sister who was of better character and used better judgment when choosing her friends. This never made me want to excel or gain insight from bad choices but rather just pulled me down further down into a pit that I could not escape. Life on the home front wasn't much different. My mom and step dad were never pleased with anything I said or did or even with and who I was becoming. I heard often "You are the eldest of the family and you are setting a bad example for your sister." However, from my perspective, the way my parents viewed my sister was the she could do no wrong.

My parents were very strict and the tighter the rope got for me, the higher I hung myself, suffocating in defeat. I also pictured God to be of the same persona, a more powerful version of my parents, and so I never tried to please Him either. I could never live up to my parents expectations, so I assumed God was somewhere up there with a big stick pointed directly at me ready to zap me in my shame every time I messed up.

Every day I went to school with knots in my stomach because at home I spent most of my time grounded and living in turmoil with my parents. I was the center of negative attention. This caused an anxiety to rise up within me. My home life made me excited to go to school, as it was an escape from my prison. In spite of this, I was never a dedicated student. When I finally made it into high school my parents had zero trust in me and so they watched me like a hawk. However, in my ninth grade year, my parents did try loosening the reigns a bit, following the advice from a family counselor, and they allowed me to attend the homecoming dance with a friend.

At that time, my parents made it very clear that I was not allowed to ride in cars, with my friends or boys, without parental supervision. However, through some devious planning, I managed to convince my parents that I would be attending this dance with a girlfriend. Really, I was dropped off at her house to meet up her and our dates. Both of our dates were seniors, and as time went on our relationships grew to be more physically intimate. This was definitely the most significant decision I'd made in my life. I didn't know then the terrible effects awaiting me because of what I had opened myself up to. This was the spot in my life where I made a turn for the worse, losing my footing and unknowingly throwing myself into captivity.

My girlfriend and I met these guys in a drafting class we were taking that year. Sometimes in the middle of the school day my girlfriend and I would leave school with our boyfriends to have lunch together and do things most fourteen year old girls wouldn't dream of. We would go our separate ways with our boyfriends to fool around in the back seats of their cars. Then a time came when my boyfriend and I ended up and at one of our houses, and one thing led to another. Before I knew it I'd compromised my sexual purity and given myself to someone who wasn't committed to me for life. I was devious and able to get home just in time to catch the automated phone call from the school informing my parents of my absence. In return, my boyfriend did the most obvious thing a guy his age would. He eventually dumped me for another girl and then graduated. It broke my heart.

Of course, when I gave into my carnal desires, I didn't even consider the consequences that were to come. Once that guy ditched me I never saw him again, or at least until I was in my mid-twenties and, thank God, only from a distance. He left me heart-broken and this only thrust me forward into the process of destroying myself. It only took that one step to open the door that brought me tumbling down an alleyway of sin. The validation I unsuccessfully sought to get at home I went elsewhere for. When I found out the power I could have over a boy just by pleasing him it gave me a false legitimacy that I chased after. It was intoxicating, like a drug that I couldn't get enough of. I didn't know then the approval I sought was available to me in Christ and I didn't have to earn that. The love God shows for His children is great and immeasurable is His forgiveness, as far as the east is from the west (Psalm 103:11-12). The Word of God says that God showed us what real love is when He sent Jesus to die for our sins (1 John 4:9-10). It says that if we put our faith in Jesus we won't perish but instead we'll have everlasting life when we leave this earth (John 3:16).

That was the year that I also began experimenting with cigarettes, marijuana and alcohol. Certainly this was all done without my parents' knowledge until one day I missed the automatic call from school. After that I was grounded for life. I had no privileges in high school, so I couldn't be a part of any sports or do any after school activities because I couldn't be trusted. I spent many years being grounded from anything enjoyable. During the colder seasons I spent lots of time in my room listening to music (when I wasn't grounded from the radio) and reading books. During the summer I spent many days circling my neighborhood on rollerblades or riding my bike because I couldn't watch TV or talk on the phone. I had no excuse for my bad behavior. I grew up in church yet I was not interested in reflecting righteousness as God's Word says that I should've. As a matter of fact, my actions were no different from someone who didn't know Jesus personally. Because I didn't read God's Word my life didn't show that I was a follower of Christ. My ignorance of His

Word may have been the cause but I didn't care in the slightest bit. I didn't know then that the only way for me to find true freedom was to find it in Christ and His Word. However, at that time I didn't realize that the confession of my need for Christ that I'd made when I was seven did me no justice as I resided in a state of outright disobedience. From my perception, I was locked up in chains with no hope of ever getting free. Therefore, to the best of my ability I struggled to conceal my bad habits from my parents to enjoy some kind of pleasure.

At that time my step-dad smoked and for a short period of time I stole cigarettes from him. He also had a change jar that he dumped quarters in when he got home from work. There were many times I went fishing in that jar for some change to buy cigarettes with. These were instances where I lied when questioned about his missing cigarettes or the quarters. I remember finding a party store close to my house that wasn't overly cautious when customers came in. I recall walking into that store at least a handful of times and swiping a cheap pack of cigarettes. I continued to smoke throughout high school and, as gross and as twisted this sounds, when I couldn't get my hands on a fresh one I would pick up the smoked butts from the ground and public ashtrays just to get a hit from one. It didn't faze me in the least bit.

Despite everything I did to poison my mind, body and spirit, the Lord still lived within me and He even spoke to me. God spoke to me in His still, small voice, although I wasn't silent enough to grasp what He was saying to me, nor did I have the knowledge to understand how God speaks to a person to reveal His purposes. Sometimes the way God communicates to us comes in the form of a thought but Satan also speaks to us through our thoughts. Something I've learned is that you have to be in God's Word to decipher who is talking to you; to understand what God's will and purpose for speaking to you is. Using His Word you can sift your thoughts to understand what lines up with it and what thoughts don't. Looking back now, I can recall a few times when God tried to speak to me but I wasn't aware that He was. It wasn't until I was in my twenties that I started learning about how God communicates to people.

The first instance that I can recall God speaking to me in the form of a thought was when we migrated to southern Michigan. God placed us in a little church in the next town for a time. While we were a part of that church I met Mike Harding. He was very different from any other guy I'd encountered. He was a respectful young man with a quiet, gentle spirit. I really didn't know him very well because he was so quiet, but he made me think that he was the kind of guy you'd want to bring home to meet your mother. He was hard to forget and from time to time his name would cross my mind, but because I was living completely out of the will of God, I made no attempt to figure out why I couldn't forget him. Mike's personality was the opposite of mine. And because of that he wasn't the kind of guy that I'd even considered messing around with. That and my bad reputation didn't mesh well with his innocent one. He was clean and careful and I was spotty and messy, or at least that's the impression I got from a distance. I couldn't discern that God had a purpose for me meeting Mike. Perhaps if I'd known to listen when the Spirit of God was speaking to me, I may not have chosen to compromise my sexual purity so young.

Thinking Question:

What is one change can you make to get out of the web of defeat, in the area you stumble?

_____

_____

_____

_____

_____

_____

_____

_____

_____

_____

_____

_____

_____

_____

_____

_____

_____

_____

_____

_____

_____

The Lie

The way of the righteous is like the first gleam of dawn, which shines ever brighter until the full light of day. But the way of the wicked is like total darkness. They have no idea what they are stumbling over

(Proverbs 4:18-19, NLT).

Just as Proverbs 4:18-19 says that those who do not follow after God's will have no idea what they're stumbling over, it was true that I had no idea what was holding me back from living the life I wanted to. I thought it was my parents' fault. The fact that they had a tight hold on me convinced me that they were literally choking the life right out of me.

As I browse through the memories from what seems like a lifetime ago, I recall wanting to be an important and influential person within my peer group. But who was I? I had no privileges like my peers did, so I could only be but a casual friend, a part-time friend that you saw at school but never really heard from outside of it. A part of me is extremely sorry that I could not take part in the fun my friends had because I simply couldn't be trusted.

Although most of the time my life was a living nightmare, surprisingly there were a few moments I enjoyed. I was involved in choir during my high school years. In tenth grade, I auditioned for the madrigal choir. Thankfully I made it in and sang in the alto section. While in this group, I did get to go on a field trip to Florida to compete in a competition. I'm really not sure why my parents allowed me to go on that trip. Based on my track record, I was consistently dishonest, and just really couldn't be trusted. It may have simply just been to alleviate the stress of having to deal with me for a short time that I was allowed the one and only privilege of attending this trip while in high school.

Eventually, even my vocal abilities became a stumbling block for me because I was very puffed up and conceited. Something I learned later in my life as true is that I can't allow just anything to be my god. That is, I have to be careful what I allow to become my sole focus. As I reflect on my past, I realize now that music and my vocal abilities became something I worshipped. Singing and music was what I spent the most time and effort in pursuing. This only led me to a dead end. Ultimately, trusting in music, myself and my talents was a big letdown. Why? Instead of being an enjoyable side in my life as an extracurricular activity, it became my every aspiration to be a better singer. It was a distraction. Not because it was a bad thing for me to be a good singer or to love music, but because *it* was what I found purpose and meaning in and that made it unhealthy. I felt validated when I could perform well and be praised for it. However, it hindered me from challenging myself to work harder in my regular classes and grasp things that I needed for future schooling.

If I'd used what then was my currency wisely, my time and resources which I had an ample supply of, I would've saved myself time and frustration later on. It came back to bite me as it cost me both time and money to learn those things in college. This ultimately was because I just didn't know how to learn. With me, myself and I on my mind I had no need for God or room for improvement in my life. I fall short of where I should be every day (Romans 3:23). When I view myself from God's standpoint, through Christ, there is more than enough grace to help me overcome my failures.

At home I was an angry, miserable individual with no one's welfare at heart except my own. I selfishly chased my own desires. Unfortunately, I sinned against my own body and lost any self respect as I fooled around with a few more guys during my high school years. As I had no privileges, I am not sure how I was able to pull this off but I did. My mindset was controlled by an inner turmoil that I couldn't understand. I was a phony, a liar, a thief, a typical Christian teenager gone pagan in search of a sense of acceptance. My life seemed as if it was crowded into a box that I was locked into, that kept me from seeing the light of day. It was also something that kept me from experiencing freedom.

The more I chased after the desires of my heart, the deeper the hole I dug became. Jesus said in His Word that, *God blesses those who realize their need for him . . . God blesses those whose hearts are pure . . .* (Matthew 5:3a, 8, NLT). I had no pure motives and certainly no relationship with God. I didn't know that what I desired and was intently searching for was actually God Himself. I remained in my ignorance, pursuing other things outside of His will. I grew up with a bad attitude. I had no self-esteem. I neither had respect for myself nor for others who disagreed with what I believed. I didn't understand that instead of trying to numb my life, as some of the people around me were doing with sex, drugs and rock and roll, I had a better option; to turn to my Savior Jesus Christ, and plead for His help. Since I had no personal relationship with Him I had no idea the power that resided within me.

Thinking Question:

What one change can you make to get out of the web of defeat in the area you stumble in? This question has a great deal of significance as it requires a person to take an honest look at oneself. Ask God for help in locating that specific area you need the most help in.

_____

_____

_____

_____

_____

_____

_____

_____

_____

_____

_____

_____

_____

_____

_____

_____

_____

_____

_____

_____

The Battle

Guard your heart above all else,
for it determines the course of your life

(Proverbs 4:23, NLT).

Growing up I never understood that the state of a person's heart is of utmost importance. Your heart will lead you if you don't lead your heart, and that's a scary thing. Sometimes your heart sends you chasing after things that seem harmless but are actually destructive. The Bible says, *the human heart is the most deceitful of all things, and desperately wicked* (Jeremiah 17:9, NLT). The book of Proverbs tells us we must keep watch over it because everything we do flows from it (4:23). It either allows you to experience freedom or keeps you from truly living a life of freedom, as Christ would have you. I wanted to experience freedom in all senses but I had no idea how. This is because once I was living in deceit I was blinded to everything that was true.

> *The LORD says, 'I will guide you along the best pathway for your life . . . Do not be like a senseless horse or mule that needs a bit and bridle to keep it under control'* (Psalm 32:8-9, NLT).

Unfortunately, I was under the impression that the true freedom I searched for could only be found if I behaved out of control. The way the people in the world grasped at *freedom* was by chasing after things and people to please themselves, no matter the cost. I know I was stuck in a cycle of chasing after things for my freedom, and just as the previous verse says I could've been compared to a senseless animal because I didn't know how to control myself. I continually made bad choices, over and over again, and it cost me the ability to do things on my own because I wasn't trustworthy. It also cost me precious time to learn how to be a responsible person.

One thing I've learned over the last 13 years is that true freedom comes with a price. You have to be willing to learn how to learn. Yes, read that again. You have to be willing to *learn how to learn*. That was something I never understood growing up. I was a repeat offender as I continuously made bad choices time after time and as a result I got stuck. I never moved forward only backwards. This led me to a place deep within my heart where I felt trapped like nothing in my life would ever change, no matter what I did. This thought held me captive and I believe that was why I refused to learn from bad decisions and make a change for the better.

Since most 17 year olds think they're invincible, many make decisions on the whim. I know I did and many around me did as well. However, just as the old saying goes, "If you play with fire you will get burned." Just before my 17th birthday, I began plotting a way out of my tortured state of controlled living. After I'd done some research, I found out that it was legal for a child to move out of their guardian's home at the age of 17. Hastily, I made arrangements to move in with a friend and planned how I would pay for my expenses once I got there. Because my dad died while my sister and I were still under 18 my mom received social security to help take care of us. Once I moved out, a portion of that check became mine. I also worked at a fast food restaurant, so that became my play money. When I lived at home and worked I couldn't even have the money that I'd earned simply because I couldn't be trusted. After I gave ten percent to the church because my mom made me, all of my money went into the bank so I never got to touch what I'd earned.

I recall coming home from school just a few days after my birthday and vulgarly announcing to my parents that I was moving out. Without delay, I threw everything I owned into cardboard boxes and plastic bags only to move basically into the neighborhood across the street. This was where my friend Nicole lived with her mom, her brother Mike, and his friend Jobo. Immediately, the cage I'd been trapped in for years was unlocked.

Nicole was a new student I'd met in choir that year. She was also someone I worked with. Nicole's plan for vacation was to go work in a summer camp as a camp counselor and so for a time, I lived at her house without her. For the first time ever, I was able to come and go from the house as I pleased with no questions asked. I had so much freedom that I had no idea how to use it responsibly. In fact, it wasn't until I moved into their house that I found out just how relaxed the atmosphere was. My perception was skewed as I thought to myself: "This was it, I'd *finally* made it!" I had no curfew, and had no problem getting my hands on some smokes thanks to some of the adults I lived with. I had money, what more did I need? Nicole's mom also smoked marijuana and so on occasion I would join her.

As I have already said, the fact that I'd compromised my sexual purity early in life led me down a road of destruction. You better believe that when I moved out it just became easier for me to dig myself into a much deeper hole. I can remember from the first time I met Nicole's brother Matt, I despised him. We'd worked together at the fast food restaurant. From my perspective, he was disgusting. We literally couldn't be around one another at work without fighting, but somehow or another Satan planned to bring us together for utter destruction. When I was living at Nicole's house, my junior year was just about over and after school was out for the summer I got involved with Matt. There were many times I would stay the night with him at his apartment. Matt's roommate, Ben, was not thrilled. Three or four years earlier I'd been put into an institution twice, for short periods of time, because I threatened suicide. It just so happened that on one of those occasions Ben and I had met.

Matt also fought with depression. He was pitiful. I didn't know until I spoke to him and got to know him better that he was beaten over the head frequently with the Bible. His parents were divorced and they came from two opposite spectrums. Some time while he was growing up his dad remarried and got custody of him and his siblings. They lived with their dad and step-mom, who were both devout Catholics, and that left him bitter because they were pretty strict. Matt's experience with church during that time wasn't a good one. My impression was that he never learned about the gracious love of God but instead heard only about God's judgment. He was thumped with a bunch of rules and religion. Eventually, he moved in with his mom who was more of a free spirit. She didn't attend church and was very lenient. I can honestly say that I probably heard more about his dad and step mom than I did about his mom. My involvement with his mom was very brief. I never really got to know who she was but I could see what she was caught up in and that it clouded her judgment. It was easy to see why he had his issues.

Matt had no self-esteem. Often he would go for days without showering. Habitually he would binge on food, smoke marijuana and drink vodka after a long day at work. Once I got involved with Matt I began to do as he did. I used to smoke a joint just so I could go to sleep. I gained a lot of weight that summer getting high and binging on food. I must've gained 20 or 30 pounds in a three month period. There were many nights I spent hanging my head over the toilet vomiting my guts out because I'd drank too much vodka. That happened all too often but somehow I never got sick enough to stop. It just goes to show you that you become like the people you surround yourself with. I'm not really even sure why I kept drinking. I wonder to this day, what was the draw? It surely didn't taste good. This was the outcome of having no self-control.

Can you imagine even while living in sin, apart from God's will for my life, God attempted to use me to speak to Matt about how he needed to know Jesus personally in order to go to Heaven? I remember frantically telling him a couple of times that he needed Jesus even though, at the time, I had no idea why. Of course, living completely out of the will of God, my words held no weight. Whenever I brought that up, he would viciously attack the name of Christ, denying that he was incomplete without Him. In his younger years Matt had spent a lot of time in church with his dad and step-mom and may very well have accepted Christ as his Savior but as he got older he did just the same as I. He grew to resent church and to rebel against anything having to do with God.

During that summer, as I destroyed myself from the inside out, I came to a place of deep depression. I didn't even hesitate to endure the pain of getting my tongue pierced, in a not-so-sanitary parlor above a laundry mat. I remember my tongue was swollen for quite a while after getting that done. I had some other piercings done at that time too, as well as a tattoo, which I believe was an external display of my inner turmoil.

I'd spoken with my mom earlier that summer about getting my car from her, which I'd saved for since I started working, but she said it wouldn't move out of her driveway until I could legally drive. When the end of the summer rolled around, I finally took my driver's test and acquired my license. I immediately went across the road and demanded the keys to my car. My mom was hesitant to hand them over but could do nothing as her hands were tied.

As the Word of God stands true in all ways, the state of a person's heart is of utmost importance because this is what either allows a person to experience freedom or keeps you from living a life of freedom in Christ: **F**reedom from lies, **R**elease from bondage, **E**xperience truth, **E**xpress peace and joy in the midst of everything, **D**on't back down, **O**vercome obstacles and **M**ake better decisions. Are you interested in finding out how to live in freedom?

Thinking Question:

Is there an instance in your life that you can recall where you made a life altering decision that took you on a turn for the worse? Describe it here:

_____

_____

_____

_____

_____

_____

_____

_____

_____

_____

_____

_____

_____

_____

_____

_____

_____

_____

_____

_____

_____

_____

The Break

The waves of death overwhelmed me; floods of destruction swept over me. The grave wrapped its ropes around me; death laid a trap in my path. But in my distress I cried out to the LORD; yes, I cried to my God for help. He heard me from his sanctuary; my cry reached his ears
(2 Samuel 22:5-7, NLT).

The month of August finally hit and school was getting ready to start up again. Over the summer I couldn't be bothered to think about my upcoming senior year. Truly, the only thing I recall contemplating as the school year was approaching was how that summer should "go out with a bang." Once my car was in my possession I drove it for about two weeks. Sometime within those two weeks reality hit.

I can recall a couple of times during that summer Nicole's mom Jane threatened to kick me out of her house because I couldn't get my rent to her on time. My rent payment had been dependent upon my mom. Unfortunately, I was at the mercy of my mom, as I had to wait for her to send it to me in the mail. The last time Jane threatened to kick me out, a fear began to rise up from deep within me. Thoughts of reality started flashing through my mind. What would I do or where would I go if I got kicked out? I am so grateful for that fear, for it caused me to go be alone and pray. I got down on my hands knees on the bathroom floor and cried out to God for help. The God whom I had neither acknowledged, nor given any control of my life to and who was of no importance to me had *finally* became my one and only hope, and by His grace I was receptive to that.

I began confessing my sin and pleading for His mercy and help. I needed a help that was beyond my control. I begged the Lord to erase the bad decisions I'd made and asked Him to give my parents the ability to forgive me. But because the desire to run away from my problems was so ingrained in me, once I was done pouring my heart out, I got off my knees and remembered that instance no more. I washed my face, left the bathroom, and then went out into the living room and got high.

Thinking Question:

Was there time in your life where you felt the need to give up and seek God's help in the midst of a sticky situation? If so, what did you do?

_____

_____

_____

_____

_____

_____

_____

_____

_____

_____

_____

_____

_____

_____

_____

_____

_____

_____

The Rescue

There is a way [that seems] right to a man,
but its end [is] the way of death

(Proverbs 16:25, NKJV).

To "end my summer with a bang," I agreed to drive to Cedar Point, an amusement park in Sandusky, Ohio. I took with me Matt, his brother Mike, and his girlfriend Shannon, who was also my age and eight months pregnant. I wasn't thinking about anyone but myself. I had no idea the power I'd just been granted when I'd gotten my driver's license and a car to get around in. At that time, whatever reality my eyes were opened to wasn't the truth because I was completely oblivious to what danger lay ahead.

After the four of us packed some things in the trunk of my car, we left for Ohio. After a long ride south we arrived at our destination and spent the day at the park. We camped out that evening and headed for home the next morning. I recall making a music video with Shannon and riding the Sky Coaster, a new ride that summer, but most of the rest of the day we spent in the park is a dream, lost in my jumbled bag of memories from that summer.

The next day, on our drive home from the park, I got lost. We went astray and ended up on a two-lane highway. The weather that day was warm at 79 degrees. The road was dry. The sky was a bit hazy but visibility on the road was clear for at least five miles. Eventually we came to an intersection with either a stop sign or a blinking red light. That day, at that particular intersection, a utility truck was parked and a crew was working on the telephone pole. I came to a complete stop, but hadn't stopped close enough to the intersection to see what was approaching. What I couldn't see as I continued north was a semi-truck headed toward us. When a truck is moving forward at a steady pace it's hard to slow down quickly. It takes time for the driver to switch gears and brake safely, slowing the momentum that is pushing the truck forward. Trying to stop a semi is like trying to stop a freight train. The driver didn't have enough time to avoid us. When I'd gone across the intersection I thought I had enough time to do it safely. Documented in the police report, the driver himself said there was one truck length between us and him when I'd crossed. He also said that he saw the front passenger in my car staring straight ahead—oblivious to what was approaching—just before the impact. As you can imagine, that semi-truck crashed into my car. The police report documented that the weight of the truck on all its axels was just short of 80,000 pounds. It t-boned my car, plowing right into the front passenger side, and it pushed us 100 yards into a bean field. The driver said that after the crash he came up to the vehicle to shut off the ignition in my car. He said he couldn't tell from the position the bodies were in who was driving the car that day. The date was August 29, 2000.

Matt was sitting in the front passenger seat that day. He wasn't wearing his seatbelt and his injuries were fatal. He was pronounced dead at the scene. He died instantly from a broken neck. As documented on the police report, he was immediately taken by the EMS to the County Health Center where the county coroner's office drew his blood and completed an autopsy on him. His family was notified of his death. He was only 19.

Shannon was seated behind Matt, in the back seat. She suffered numerous injuries. Recall that she was eight months pregnant. Because of where she was seated in the car, her body withstood a tremendous amount of force. Had her son Tyler been born that day under regular circumstances, he would've been healthy but instead he took the brunt of that force for her and lost his life. That meant that if she hadn't been pregnant she may have died too! The impact the truck had on the car made it sort-of fold together, like a piece of foil. The car caved into itself from the top and the sides, more so where Shannon was seated. After being trapped in the car for nearly 40 minutes, Shannon's heart stopped. The police and rescue team had to literally tear the roof off the car to retrieve her. They resuscitated her using CPR but broke several of her ribs in the process. She was then airlifted to a local hospital. Her shoulder, leg, pelvis and both hands were shattered. Her bladder was torn. She also suffered a head injury. During the time she was trapped in the car, her left foot had been firmly planted on top of the catalytic converter, and was so badly burned the doctors took skin from her thigh to save her toes. The worst part was that she had to bury her baby boy.

Seated next to Shannon was Mike. He also had extensive issues to deal with. The police report documented that after the accident he had been air lifted by Life Flight to a different local hospital. The tip of his left pelvis broke off and was plated back on and it was fractured in three other places as well. There was water on his lungs and the doctors drained them. He was put on bed rest for four weeks straight, while his pelvis healed. Afterward, he underwent physical therapy to learn how to walk again because his muscles had deteriorated so much while on bed rest. He stayed in the hospital for five weeks and two days. He was released from the hospital just one day before Shannon.

At the scene of the accident I was comatose and remained in that state for a total of ten days. The injuries I suffered were internal, but affected me externally. I was also air lifted by Life Flight to the same hospital as Mike. I'd bruised some of my ribs, probably from the force of hitting the steering wheel. I can remember for quite a while after that I could feel a pain in my ribs right before it rained. My right lung collapsed and I'd suffered a severe head injury. My mom said that the hospital I'd been taken to in Ohio had been treating me with Penicillin by IV. I'm allergic to Penicillin and I had a reaction that made my entire body swell up. Had my mom not realized this the Penicillin might've killed me. Once my mom figured out what was happening, I was immediately transferred to a hospital closer to my home. I had a tracheotomy, which is a tube, stuck into my throat to help me breathe. This affected how my vocal chords worked and so my voice no longer sounded the way it once did. I had a feeding tube stuck into my stomach to nourish me, as well as a catheter stuck into my side to empty the waste out of my body while I lay incapacitated. Because my right lung collapsed they had to open up part of my back and do surgery to repair that. While they were fixing my lungs, I was really fortunate that the doctors decided to scrape the tar out of them that had accumulated from smoking cigarettes. After a three month stay in the hospital, just before Thanksgiving, I was released and went home with my family.

I did not return to school right away. Instead, I spent a year at a rehabilitation center in a day program. A company my insurance paid for would pick me up from home every morning and take me to the city of Birmingham for my rehabilitation. Then, in the afternoon when I was finished therapy for the day they'd bring me home.

While in therapy I worked with many therapists. A physical therapist I saw helped me to relearn the simplest tasks. I had to strengthen my hands and arms by stacking blocks, my muscles by exercising, and lifting small weights. I had to relearn how to balance myself to walk safely. I remember having to watch my feet as I was walking so that I would walk in a straight line and not run into people or walls. I had to do this to walk up and down the stairs for many years. For a time, I walked like Frankenstein. My family to this day still picks on me for that. I remember when I'd get up to walk it felt like I weighed a million pounds. It was a lot of weight for my knees to tolerate even though, as you can imagine, I'd lost a lot of weight in the hospital because the only nourishment my body was getting was from a feeding tube. It was hard to balance myself and hold myself up straight. I also had to practice turning my head from side-to-side. That was the most painful part of physical therapy. After lying in a hospital bed for three months, I couldn't turn my head at all. When I attempted to do so I experienced a jolt of pain that would go through my neck. My therapist worked on rotating my head while tipping it up and down, and little by little, it stretched my neck muscles. After some months I was able to turn my head completely from one side to the other without pain. She helped me to regain the movement of my body.

I had to work with several other therapists to get myself back to myself. A speech therapist used flip books to help me relearn how to read words and to identify items in pictures. It was as if I'd started school all over again learning the basics. I worked on my writing and speaking, at a very slow pace, as I couldn't retain most of anything I worked on understanding. I had to relearn my A,B,C's and 1, 2, 3's along with my elementary comprehension skills.

I worked with two different occupational therapists that helped me to relearn how to do responsibilities both at home and in a work setting. Practicing things such as cooking meals, cleaning, washing dishes or folding laundry; perform simple chores to work on my hand-eye coordination. They also tried to help me learn how to deal with my emotions, in both types of settings, in order to strengthen my ability to function independently.

I also worked with a recreational therapist who helped me find things to do to enjoy myself. She worked with me on how to do leisurely activities. This was where I picked up my love for the card game Uno. She helped me learn to enjoy myself by playing board games, exercising by shooting hoops, relearning how to ride my bike, and rollerblade. (I worked with a home recreational therapist for a time after I got discharged from my day rehab program. She worked with me at my house practicing these same skills as well as working on my driving skills.)

In addition to the physical and cognitive effects, my head injury effected my emotions, too. For example, I would smile at inappropriate times, like when I was given some of kind of bad news, like someone had died or during instances when someone was scolding me. Instead of crying I would smile. I also had to learn the difference between what was appropriate behavior for my work place and at home as well as what wasn't. Unfortunately, over many years I learned the hard way how to lose a job because I couldn't focus well enough to really understand my job. There were many times I got frustrated and didn't know how to express that. Sometimes I went to the point of breaking down and losing my temper or I'd give up and wouldn't even do my job at a satisfactory level.

That January, following my release from the hospital, after rehab, I had a special education teacher who came to my house and home schooled me for the first half of my senior year. With my teacher I practiced the basic skills of reading, writing and math. My second semester didn't happen until the following school year. When I returned to school my curriculum consisted of special education classes that earned my needed credits to graduate. I was really blessed because I did so only a semester late.

In the months that followed the accident, I saw an ENT, or ear, nose and throat doctor, who conducted some tests on me and told me that my vocal chords had become lazy. He wrote me a prescription for voice therapy and so I went to Oakland University and worked with a vocal instructor, who was actually an opera singer. I never really followed through with the vocal exercises that she gave me to help improve the tone and strength of my voice, so consequently I never regained the use of my original speaking or singing voice.

On my own, I studied how people communicated with one another. I thought it so odd that when people would greet each other, one person would ask another how they were doing, but only in passing, so they wouldn't even stick around to hear the answer. I made many mistakes in learning how to talk with others and embarrassed myself plenty of times but somehow the Lord taught me how to have a conversation with someone; this time in a more respectful manner.

I was shy and unsure of myself but I have to believe that it was because of His nudge that I began approaching people to share what God had done for them by sending Jesus to die on the cross for their sins. It was sort of like God had rewired my brain, so much so in fact, that He was the only One I wanted to talk about. Unfortunately, not many people felt the same way. I had very few friends and I offended the ones I did have many times over. I expressed my disapproval of many things I'd once thought were ok. I was very vocal about my beliefs and many times pushed my convictions on others to the extreme until I learned I couldn't speak in such a way and honor God at the same time. That lesson took me many, many years to learn.

Roughly two years after my car accident, I started having seizures. I had them mostly at work or in my sleep and I had them often enough that against my mother's wishes my neurologist decided to medicate me. He treated me with two different seizure medications that I took throughout the day. One of the medications I took was the same one prescribed to my dad when he alive. Over the next eight years, I was heavily medicated for epilepsy during the day and eventually with another medication at night. Even though I was heavily medicated I wasn't completely seizure free. My meds kept my head in the clouds, so much so that I had difficulty keeping a job because my attention span was pretty bad and my short term memory was even worse. I couldn't follow the simplest instructions without asking my bosses to repeat themselves over and over again.

At some jobs I even tried taking notes but that never helped. I lost quite a few jobs because I just could not get them down. I tried at least one medication for the A.D.D. I dealt with but nothing was ever successful in helping me with that.

Somehow, by God's grace, I was able to finish high school and go on to college. I learned how to read and write like a college student, although I had the mental capacity to understand very little and to absorb information even less. I was blessed to have passed all of my classes in a community college and eventually earned my Associates Degree. I'm not going to even tell you how long that took. I am currently working on earning my certification in Biblical Studies. My life verse is from 2 Corinthians 12:9, which says . . . *My grace is all you need. My power works best in weakness. So now I am glad to boast about my weaknesses, so that the power of Christ can work through me* (NLT). It's amazing, the more closely I've held onto that verse the more I've seen the power of Christ do something in my life that was beyond me; in my schooling, at work, in my relationships, and in my involvement in ministry.

The semi-truck that changed my life is a metaphor of what the world will do to you if you let it. My pastor often states that the world is like a car in that will run you over and not hit the brakes. For some people it would only take a car accident to wake them up, but I figure because I was so bull-headed, it took something much bigger for me to see that I was traveling on the wrong path headed for destruction.

Thinking Question:

What about you? Do you have something that you fight with, a bad habit, or something that holds you back from growing passed that failure and moving on to bigger and better things?

The Affects

Many are the plans in a man's heart, but it is the LORD's purpose that prevails

(Proverbs 19:21, NIV).

After my car accident many things were affected in me. The thing that I'd worshipped for so long had been taken away; my idol was smashed to pieces. This idol was my singing voice. After I had the breathing tube in my throat, my voice was changed forever. In high school, my desire was to go to college for music to become a high school choir teacher. My high school teacher had inspired me to be like him. However, once I'd lost my voice my teaching dream was crushed. It took me many years to deal with the loss of my voice. I grew up in a family full of musicians. My grandfather was a renowned Gospel singer. I'd trained my voice when I was a kid, and so I had a very large singing range. I'd also played instruments while growing up but the satisfaction I got was nothing compared to the way I felt when I was singing my heart out, both in choir and on my own. I grew up singing and once I lost that ability I really didn't know who I was. My identity was lost or so I thought.

I also suffered a brain injury, which was absolutely devastating. I've heard that when your brain is injured it can heal itself—with the Lord's help of course. I honestly had no idea how great my recovery had actually been until I'd stopped taking the seizure medication that was prescribed to me for many years. I'd gone to the doctor to have my blood drawn and when the results came back the nurse called to say that the numbers in my liver were off. I guess I should've been aware that the medication I'd been taking all those years could cause long term damage to my liver but honestly I didn't know. When I got that call things started to change. My mom and I started doing some research before I saw my doctor again. He tested me for epilepsy, giving me an EEG which read my brain waves, and nothing showed to be abnormal. As a result, I got a reluctant ok from the doctor to begin weaning myself off of my medications. Sometime later I started seeing a new doctor who treated my epilepsy with a drug that wouldn't interfere with my daytime functionality, but has kept me seizure free for a longer amount of time than I'd ever been before. I started taking a medication at night which allowed me to be clear-minded during the day. At this point, I haven't had a seizure for at least three years.

The summer I turned 17 and moved out was bittersweet for me. I experienced more adventure than I had ever before, as I got a taste of what unbridled freedom was like. I also demonstrated stupidity beyond measure but thank God for hindsight because since that time I've learned more from that summer than I had in my entire life.

> *Remember that in a race everyone runs, but only one person gets the prize. You also must run in such a way that you will win. All athletes practice strict self-control. They do it to win a prize that will fade away, but we do it for an eternal prize. So I run straight to the goal with purpose in every step. I am not like a boxer who misses his punches. I discipline my body like an athlete, training it to do what it should. Otherwise, I fear that after preaching to others I myself might be disqualified* (1 Corinthians 9:24-27, NLT).

Thinking Question:

Are there any tough lessons you have had to go through? If so, have you asked God to reveal why you went through that and what you were supposed to learn from that?

_____

_____

_____

_____

_____

_____

_____

_____

_____

_____

_____

_____

_____

_____

_____

_____

_____

_____

_____

_____

_____

_____

The Next Season

For I know the plans I have for you," declares the LORD, "plans to prosper you and not to harm you, plans to give you hope and a future
(Jeremiah 29:11, NIV).

After my accident I had one friend, Aimee, who was a Christian and stuck around. She came to my house often and would pick me up to go out for coffee, as I couldn't drive myself anywhere for at least the first year after my accident. She was someone I'd met years earlier when my family moved south and found a church to attend. It was at that same church that I'd also met Mike Harding. Once when Aimee came over for a visit she brought him with her.

Mike was that very same guy that I couldn't ever forget after meeting. Over the years his name went through my head many times and I never understood why. This is an instance where if I would've taken the time to seek out God's reasons for why I couldn't forget him, I may have saved myself some trouble. However, when I met him this time, I fell head over heels for him. He was so very different from any other guy I'd been attracted to. He was a quiet, soft spoken person, who chose his words carefully. He was observant, more of a spectator than a participant, who definitely didn't want to be the center of attention.

Prior to this time, Mike had been on his search for freedom traveling with some friends around the country doing some crazy things. As a result, he dealt with a drug problem that, metaphorically speaking, sent him into "the wilderness." Unfortunately, this problem followed him right out of that experience. He'd been brought up in a home that did things very opposite of mine. His parents trusted him and so he rode his bike wherever he wanted to go. He went to Christian concerts with his family. He went to Christian schools while he was growing up. He also went to church regularly and his parents were actively involved in serving at church. While he was growing up he'd felt as if he was sheltered from everything. So when he became "of age" he went searching for what he thought he'd missed out on, but unfortunately he had met up with a fake, a mere pacifier, that would become a stronghold to battle with in his adult years.

Over the next year, we spent lots of time talking and getting to know each other. Eventually, I told him how I felt about him and so we did something neither of us had ever done before, we courted. We did not kiss and we were not physically intimate. We just spent a lot of time together talking and getting to know each other. We prayed together, read and memorized God's Word together. We even did Bible study for a time with a family member of mine who had recently accepted Jesus into his heart. I also helped Mike get a job at the fast food restaurant where I worked.

Well, sometime within that year of courtship Mike ran into some old buddies who he'd previously used drugs with. In that year since I'd reconnected with him, he stayed clean but unfortunately once he met up with his old friends, he fell prey to temptation and got high. He was honest with me about that and the only thing I knew to do was go to my parents to see if they could recommend some help. However, after what my parents had gone through because of my stupid decisions just a couple of years earlier, they decided I could no longer see Mike. I was heartbroken. As a result, I spent much time on my knees in prayer, pleading with God for Mike.

After we broke up, Mike lived with his parents for about a year and then he joined the Navy. He went through boot camp and ended up in Washington State. Right around that same time, I'd moved out of my parents' home and gotten an apartment with a girlfriend from church, in hopes of seeing Mike before he left. However, I just missed seeing him before he left for the Navy. I continued to pray for him but after some time I did date someone else. It was not until I allowed myself to get completely side-tracked with this person that I woke up and remembered that hope I had for God to restore Mike and bring him back to me. God reminded me that I had to flee from my sin and get myself right with Him before anything could change for the better in my life. For this reason, I made the necessary decision and broke up with that person and then I did some more praying and waiting.

> 2-15-03
>
> ## Yet to Be
> I'd like to think I know you love
> I'd like to think you care
> But when I think of how
> I know it isn't fair we're drifting
> I wish that I could see the future
> And see that we'll be fine
> The past is often one fine
> Teaching me you'll soon be mine teacher
> I know requardless of what I think
> God controls my life
> He knows my every twitch & blink
> And He's prepared a wife.
> So as I think of you & me,
> I know the best is
> yet to be.
>
> Mike

About two years went by and Mike came home from the Navy early. He'd experienced a breakdown and had been treated for depression. Unfortunately, he'd also fallen prey to his old habits and this resulted in him getting discharged from the Navy. When he arrived home, I eagerly met up with Mike only to find him discouraged and so very different. It was amazing what his experience in the Navy had done to him. I'm not saying anything derogatory about the Navy. It just isn't the right choice for everyone. He was broken, not the same guy I'd met years earlier. He was in need of some Spiritual healing. In the year after he returned I spent some more one-on-one time with him. As I pursued Mike, God brought him back around and he desired to have more than a friendship with me. We dated for a year and then we decided to get married.

Of course, my parents weren't thrilled with the idea, so when the talk of marriage came around they would have nothing to do with it. As we pursued the idea of marriage Mike and I sought Spiritual guidance from some trusted godly leaders. We also took Bible studies together to seek God for wisdom in this decision. Eventually, my dad's family took on the responsibility of putting on our wedding. Mike's parents also gave us some money to help. At that time my aunt Patty was a wedding planner and she had a business partner and a very good friend named Diane, who is a nationally renowned cake designer. My grandfather had taken leadership as the pastor of that small church I'd grown up in and where most of my dad's church-going family attended. My aunt Patty gave me her wedding dress, which was fitted by a woman in the church for me to wear. In November, right around Thanksgiving, my grandfather married us in that little church. My dad's family made a potluck dinner for our reception and Diane made us a beautiful wedding cake as a gift. Everything was perfect, as it was my dream-come-true. Well . . . almost.

Thinking Question:

Is there something you're waiting to see fulfilled in your life? What are you doing as you wait? What are you holding onto for hope as you wait?

_____

_____

_____

_____

_____

_____

_____

_____

_____

_____

_____

_____

_____

_____

_____

_____

_____

_____

The Adventure

Jesus answered, 'I am the way and the truth and the life. No one comes to the Father except through me'

(John 14:6, NIV).

Mike took up the trade of truck driving when he came home from the Navy, so once we got married, I didn't hesitate to travel with him. For the first eight months of that year, we traveled weekly in his truck all over the United States and were home on the weekends. We didn't actually "live" anywhere we just stayed with family when we came home. Eventually, we decided to switch trucking companies for the remainder of our time on the road together. That year, we were on the road three to four weeks at a time and home for a few days a month. However, since only my outer circumstances changed when I got on the road with Mike, I still had a lot of strongholds that were very alive and active inwardly. I'm referring to the bad habits that were a strong force in my inner self, being expressed in the form of anger and unforgiveness. For instance, when we came into town, we'd take turns staying with his parents and then with mine.

In that time, I managed to hurt my mom and step-dad repeatedly with my words. So much so in fact, that my mom said we were no longer welcome to stay at their house when we came home. This hurt me deeply, and God opened my eyes and allowed me to see that I was also hurting my husband with my words. That was when I realized this was a battle that I couldn't overcome on my own. In fact, when I still lived with my parents I'd always denied the fact that I had a problem expressing myself in a respectful manner. However, once the Lord allowed me to see that I was hurting the very person I'd spent many years pleading with God for, the only thing left for me to do was to fight this spiritual battle God's way. So I tried something I'd never done before. I pulled out my weapon, which in the Bible the writer of Ephesians refers to as the "Sword of the Spirit" (Ephesians 6). I can't remember how I came upon this thought but I decided to find specific Scriptures that dealt with the bad habits I was fighting with. These were the areas in my mind and my heart that needed to be fixed.

Because we were fortunate to have had wireless internet in our truck, it gave me opportunity to get into and study God's Word using some great online Biblical resources. I started with studying topics like "anger," and "words." I found God's Word full of wisdom concerning these topics and others. I began digging deep into God's Word concerning the things that needed to be excavated from my mind and heart. I studied Scriptures on speaking with grace, the power of my words and my attitude, and I started seriously considering what I was thinking about. I also searched the Scriptures to find and plant good things inside of my mind and heart, such as compassion, kindness, humility, gentleness and patience (Colossians 3:12). The Holy Spirit would lead me to just the right verses which I wrote down on 3x5 cards and taped up on the glove box in front of me, so that I could read them every day. I spent at least eight hours a day sitting in that seat, constantly reading the Scripture and memorizing it. As a matter of fact, I taped up new verses on a regular basis concerning self-control and anger management from God's perspective. This was the only thing that could break through the bondage of anger that held me captive. This helped me greatly as God took my mouth and my thoughts and rewired me, renewing my mind and heart with His Word. Even during my time of loneliness in that truck, I have to admit that it was probably the best time in my Spiritual life for God to do so much transformation on inside of me.

During that time, I took some college Bible classes online and through the mail. Eventually, though, I grew very lonely, as I needed the companionship of other Christians. I grew weary of traveling so much and so we got off the road. When we did Mike found a job changing oil in a small shop close to our home. Right away, we got into an apartment and I taped Scripture to my living room walls. God always sat me in the right seat in order to see the Scripture I needed to read, at just the right time. That was a tough time for us in our marriage, as money was tight and Mike was drawn once again to using his drug of choice but we made it through that valley and learned a lot. We eventually rented a house connected to our landlord's home so that the cost of living was much more manageable. Mike got cleaned up and eventually got a local trucking job, which is what he desired to do most. I started working part-time in a school district and picked up caregiving.

Thinking Question:

Is there any habit that you've been stumbling over that you could consider digging into God's Word for some help in conquering? If so, find that word in the back of your Bible or use online Bible resources to find Scripture to help and do the same thing I did. First write the verses down and put them somewhere you'll see them every day. Maybe you'll tape your to the mirror or put them up on your bedroom walls, read them and memorize them. Do whatever it takes.

_____

_____

_____

_____

_____

_____

_____

_____

_____

_____

_____

_____

_____

_____

_____

_____

_____

The Truth

*Jesus Christ is the same yesterday
and today and forever*

(Hebrews 13:8, NIV).

Even after I've turned my life over to God I still fight an inner battle everyday between choosing to do what I *feel* is good, or choosing to do what I *know* is right, based upon God's Word. Anyone who enters into a relationship with God will fight this battle, while here on this earth, and it's an outright lie if anyone tells you otherwise. Most would agree that this life isn't a cake walk. Sometimes bad things come our way even when we make the right choices and there may be nothing we can do about them. Other times, bad things happen because of poor choices we've made. Something that always remains the same no matter the issues or consequences we face is that, God is God and nothing you or I do will ever change that fact. God is entirely into you. He loves you more than you can understand. When everyone in your life abandons you and everything you hold onto so tightly crumbles God is still there ready and waiting. He loves you so much and has some great plans for your life. If there is one thing we can take to the bank with certainty, it is that the Lord can and will use those hard times in each of our lives for our good, if we allow Him to (Romans 8:28). He can build you up even when you're broken from your circumstances, when things in your life dissolve. He uses those instances to allow you to see your need for Him. This is when you can experience Him working the most in you if you allow Him to.

Something I spent many years avoiding was unforgiveness. I am very fortunate to have learned in my adult years the importance of what *true* forgiveness is and how to extend it. Something I've been learning in my marriage is a better understanding of giving and receiving forgiveness. God's Word says we are not to let the sun go down when we're angry, so that we avoid giving the Devil any power to inhabit our lives (Ephesians 4:26-27). In the past, I harbored bitterness and resentment in my heart against people who I felt wronged me and this didn't do me any favors. In fact, it held me back from becoming all that I could be. It created a tangled mess on the inside of me that trapped me and kept me down in a pit.

If someone were to ask me what life means, I would answer that it is living for Christ. It's not about making the most money, buying the latest gadgets, or having the best of the best. Some would say I have my head in the sand but the truth is, chasing after things leads to an empty life and it definitely doesn't lead to freedom. If that were the purpose of life then there wouldn't be any hope for anyone, either here on earth or in eternity. I had to learn that truth the hard way. I thought I could make it through this life without His help but that brought me to my knees pleading for His mercy. By God's grace I am here as a testimony. He spared my life and gave me a second chance to live in accordance with His ways; the safest place to remain is there.

> *Look straight ahead, and fix your eyes on what*
> *lies before you. Mark out a straight path for your*
> *feet; stay on the safe path. Don't get sidetracked;*
> *keep your feet from following evil*
> (Proverbs 4:25-27, NLT).

Thinking Question:

Is there anything you avoid dealing with in your life? If so why? What holds you back from confronting those issues?

_____

_____

_____

_____

_____

_____

_____

_____

_____

_____

_____

_____

_____

_____

_____

_____

_____

_____

_____

_____

_____

_____

_____

The Burden
or Is it?

Do not be deceived: God cannot be mocked.
A man reaps what he sows

(Galatians 6:7, NIV).

Because of my actions 13 years ago I have a life-long consequence that I deal with. Due to the head injury I suffered I have epilepsy. This is what I refer to as a thorn in my flesh. The Apostle Paul wrote of one in the Bible that he dealt with himself in 2 Corinthians 12. This thorn was a splinter, which the Bible calls a tormentor of Satan that Paul had to deal with to keep him humble after the life changing truth he'd received from God Himself. I can very much understand the frustration he had with his thorn. I don't deal with the pain of my thorn on a daily basis as I am medicated for it, but from time to time it rears its ugly head and stops me from being productive, or so I think, and going about my daily life as it strips away my driving privileges for a time. Sometimes when that happens it's almost like I feel chained up. The burden of epilepsy has its moments when it gets me down, and tempts me to give up but God is faithful to uphold me in those times. Depending on how I view those circumstances God will often teach me the most about my need for Him during those times if I allow Him to.

August of 2011 was, in fact, the end of a very long six-month period of not driving after having a seizure. That time around, I went through a period of depression that no one except God and my husband knew I was fighting. Not too long after that, I was grateful that God broke through in my heart and mind, and brought down the walls to save me in my brokenness.

Don't be tricked into believing that everything will be great when you grow up or become "of age" and can make your own decisions. There are many battles you will have yet to fight in your adult years. The time is *now* to prepare to fight those battles, by learning how to learn from your mistakes.

The summer of 2011 when I couldn't drive, I was invited to attend a women's conference with some ladies from my church and God spoke directly to me. The speaker discussed the desert I'd found myself wondering in for quite some time. She also spoke about preparation and finishing unfinished tasks. The impression I got from this was that it was time to pack up and move out of my desert. As a matter of fact, right in the middle of her talking about finishing unfinished tasks she stopped, looked directly into the audience and said, "There is a woman here who has been working on a book and God says you need to finish it." So here I am completing my unfinished tasks and I'm not overwhelmed but excited and thankful! I'm telling you all this to encourage you to see that *this* is possible for you too. *You* can also experience God working in you and around you, for your good, even while you're in a pit (Romans 8:28).

Thinking Question:

Where do you find yourself today? Are you wandering in a place of uncertainty or a place of despair with no hope of the future? What can you do to turn your thinking around? Why not try what I've already suggested and get into God's Word to find some encouraging truths to hang on to?

_____

_____

_____

_____

_____

_____

_____

_____

_____

_____

_____

_____

_____

_____

_____

_____

_____

_____

_____

_____

_____

14

The Battle

The purposes of a person's heart are deep waters,
but one who has insight draws them out

(Proverbs 20:5, NIV).

As I reflect on all God has brought me through, I am reminded of that crucial moment that took place 13 years ago on the bathroom floor when I cried out to God for help in the midst of my battle. The Bible tells of many people who experienced the same thing. For example, David cried out to God many times for His help in uncertain circumstances. The account in the Bible that hits closest to home for me is found in 2 Samuel 22. This is a praise David wrote after he battled his fifth giant. He proclaimed:

> *The LORD is my rock, my fortress, and my savior; my God is my rock, in whom I find protection. He is my shield, the power that saves me, and my place of safety. He is my refuge, my savior, the one who saves me from violence* (vs. 2-3, NLT).

The Scripture says the battle was fierce when David called on God to deliver him from his enemies.

In the Bible he wrote about his experience saying that the waves of death covered him, and destruction terrified him; the pains of hell surrounded him and then the lure of death was provoking. In the midst of all of David's ruin God stopped and listened to his cry for help (2 Samuel 22:4-7).

What God did for David, He can do for you and me, too. In just the same way as David experienced God's hand of redemption, God also turned to me when I reached out for him in my time of greatest need. That same comfort is available to you to grab a hold of. It was almost like I got to experience God's hand of grace saving me, just as David did:

> *Then the earth quaked and trembled. The foundations of the heavens shook; they quaked because of his anger. Smoke poured from his nostrils; fierce flames leaped from his mouth. Glowing coals blazed forth from him. He opened the heavens and came down; dark storm clouds were beneath his feet . . . The LORD thundered from heaven; the voice of the Most High resounded . . . He reached down from heaven and rescued me; he drew me out of deep waters* (2 Samuel 22:8-10, 14 & 17, NLT).

I am reminded of the giants I've battled over the years that have hung around my life, holding me captive. For a time, I dealt with the giants of substance abuse and sexual sin, which actually were the ripple effects of me not dealing with root of my problem of anger. It was anger and the denial of it which turned into bitterness that held me prisoner. The giant of bitterness had a spiraling effect on the rest of my life. It opened me up to be easy prey for other giants' pursuits. And if God would have allowed it to, could've brought end to my life here on earth.

Something I've learned is that bondage comes in all shapes and forms. Every one of us has some kind of bondage we face at different times in our lives, whether or not we are aware of it. Yes, I was fortunate to have had my slate wiped clean and given a fresh start to life after I had my accident. This doesn't mean I don't have any battles that I face today. I combat between good and evil every day. Although I don't generally battle the same things I did 13 years ago, the giants I face now come in different forms. In fact, over the years some of those things that have been my worst battles I've found I can use to my advantage. For instance, my stubbornness I believe is a gift from God. When I was younger I continuously tripped over it because I never learned how to develop it into something useful. Instead of helping me to stick to my beliefs and hold to right things, it made me hard-headed and unable to learn from my mistakes because I thought that the problem was with everyone else who disagreed with me and my decisions. When I grew up though, I found that the problem was actually in me. Now, instead of allowing my stubbornness to be a stumbling block, I use it to my advantage. God has reshaped that block and sharpened me to be persistent during battles, using His Word.

Because Christ says that it will not be until I reach heaven that my battles will disappear, I will keep my guard up (1 Peter 5). The Bible says the enemy prowls around like a lion looking for a person he can consume (1 Peter 5:8). Lions are sneaky, crafty and very good at catching their prey. Their very lives depend upon this skill. I believe that is why Satan is compared to this animal. He's devious, cunning and very good at pouncing on his prey which is both you and I. That is why I believe it is important for us to take an honest look at ourselves from God's perspective. Satan can have us tangled up in our own desires and keep us from experiencing the freedom that we were meant to. As long as we're bound up by Satan and his plans for our lives, we won't be able to see the great plans God has for us.

I share my story with hopes that if you're struggling with how things are going in your life and you feel hopeless, that I can encourage you to find hope not in what's going on around you, good or bad, but in Jesus. The Bible is full of reasons why Jesus is *always* the answer to your problems; telling of who He is and how much He loves you. The Bible says *Jesus Christ is the same yesterday, today and forever* (Hebrews 13:8, NIV). Unlike the circumstances around us, *He does not change like shifting shadows* (James 1:17, NIV). He loves you with an everlasting love and nothing can ever separate you from that love (Psalm 103:17, Romans 8:35-39). His plans for you are great (Jeremiah 29:11). He is the one that can lead you to live in safety (Psalm 4:8). He will shelter you beneath His wings and you can find refuge in Him, the midst of any battle your facing (Psalm 91:4). Once you're His He will never leave you nor forsake you (Deuteronomy 31:6). That's a lot of promises, written just for you to hang onto.

Something that can get in the way of my perception is me, myself and I. Only I can choose to ask the Lord to help me see what is wrong with me or to show me the faults that I am not aware of. God can open my eyes to the truth and I can accept that or I can choose to ignore it. If you took a look deep within yourself, you might find that battle within yourself too. True freedom will be ours once we deal with the undesirable things that lurk within us or when we make ourselves available to God to do a work within us that is beyond ourselves (John 8:32).

Thinking Question:

So what about you? What areas in your life are coming to mind that need change? Whatever it is will require from you much courage.

The Value of Learning

Commit your actions to the Lord
and your plans will succeed

(Proverbs 16:3).

A lesson that God seems to have been teaching me more so in the last few years is on self-control. I've found that if I can't honestly see a need in my life for God to work on the inside of me it's always linked to an issue much bigger than the problem itself, such as self-control. This again touches on the importance of getting to the root of the problem.

Self-control is the ability to show restraint. It also takes self-control to be still enough to face the issues head on instead of running away from them. As a teenager self-control wasn't evident in my life. I spewed words in anger and negativity constantly. When you're young you tend to pick up the habits of your parents, both good and bad. I'm not pointing fingers, just stating a universal truth. Kids mimic their parents' actions and words. In my mom's younger years, she had a bad habit of also spewing negativity out of her mouth. I'm not sure why my sister never picked that bad habit too but I battled with my mouth for many, many years. Now that I'm grown I don't blame my mom for my faults, but instead recognize them and do my part to build myself up stronger in those areas. True freedom simply comes from opening God's Word, reading it and learning it. This allows you to experience God doing a work in you that is beyond yourself.

The Bible also has a lot to say about the power of our words. Our words can be used as weapons that we can hurt others with or can be used as tools extending grace: *Do not let any unwholesome talk come out of your mouths, but only what is helpful for building others up according to their needs, that it may benefit those who listen* (Ephesians 4:29, NLT). You can usually tell a lot about a person just by the way they talk. In the Bible, Luke wrote in his book: *The good man brings good things out of the good stored up in his heart, and the evil man brings evil things out of the evil stored up in his heart. For out of the overflow of his heart his mouth speaks* (Luke 6:45, NIV). I know when self-control is evident in my life. It is reflected in my speech and affects my relationships with others, and the same thing stands true for you. However, this does not mean that we will ever reach perfection, on this side of eternity anyhow. Some of us, myself included will always have the struggle of trying to muzzle our mouths while others will not. For example, my husband is the most laid-back person you would ever meet. He and I are opposites. He's a quiet, sensitive, thoughtful, observant person while I have a big mouth and would rather be assertive by speaking up, sometimes in a not so delicate way. God has used my husband to teach me about thinking before I speak. In the Bible there are many verses on choosing your words wisely. *Even fools are thought wise when they keep silent; with their mouths shut, they seem intelligent* (Proverbs 17:28, NLT). That verse and many others have taught me so much about considering my words. They've helped me become a better communicator and taught me how to speak with grace and mercy.

Satan the deceiver, can put a mask over our eyes so that we aren't looking at ourselves truthfully. If we don't see our faults then we can't ask God for His help to make the changes we need to in order to experience freedom to fullest. I cannot stress enough the importance of storing God's Word up in our hearts, that is, reading it and memorizing it. We do this all the time with songs and books and movies. So why not try opening the Bible and learning it? It is so vital in order to experience victory over the bondage that keep us stunted in our lives and enjoy freedom from those things. I have found the closer I am to Christ, the more imperfections I can see in myself, but it's also true that there is more grace available for me to take hold of. This is where I leave off and allow the Holy Spirit to do His work in changing me from the inside out.

I find it interesting in the Gospels that Jesus taught using parables, or metaphors, referring to nature in order to depict the inner life of a person. Just as in nature there are certain things we can do in our lives in order to reap a great harvest and enjoy the consequences of good things living in us and coming out of us. On the other hand, just as a garden can be ruined and overtaken by weeds, you and I can also experience the toxicity of allowing our cravings to be what we chase after. You can either flourish or wither; that decision is yours. This spiritual truth struck a chord in me while I was weeding my vegetable garden last year: deal with an issue before it deals with you. Basically, to get out of a rut you have to get to the root of the problem. Just the same as weeding my garden if I don't pull those weeds out from the root they'll spring up quicker and overtake my garden. Turning this around into a practical application for your life simply means that when you're made aware of a fault that exists within yourself, you can't just ignore it. Along with prayer, you must get into God's Word to search for help in overcoming that issue. This was something I avoided doing while growing up, and it laid the pattern for my future, which followed me out of my adolescence and into adulthood. If you've heard everything that I've said so far, maybe you can consider *this* time in your life as preparation for your future, no matter your age.

> *I will walk about in freedom, for I have*
> *sought out your precepts*
> (Psalm 119:45, NIV).

Thinking Question:

What are you doing to prepare for your future? Are there any valuable lessons you've learned that make you better prepared to handle your adulthood responsibly? Is there anything you can do to improve your learning skills?

_____

_____

_____

_____

_____

_____

_____

_____

_____

_____

_____

_____

_____

_____

_____

_____

_____

_____

_____

The Focus

It is for freedom that Christ has set us free.
Stand firm, then, and do not let yourselves
be burdened again by a yoke of slavery.

(Galatians 5:1, NIV)

Some priceless wisdom my grandfather told me while growing up was this: "Every decision that you make will affect you for the rest of your life." Basically, you're choosing today what you would have for tomorrow. All of us fail at meeting this every day but thank God each day is a fresh start, filled with a fresh portion of His grace to try again. I didn't appreciate my grandfather's wisdom until I was much older. The choices I made 13 years ago cost the lives of a young man and an unborn baby boy. I also put myself and two other people in danger of losing their lives. I share this story with you so that you might consider the path you're taking. Is it leading you the way of meaningful purpose allowing you to experience freedom or is it made of instant gratification that sends you plummeting deeper into a pit?

Something I didn't realize in my youth was that Christ was and still is the only solution to my problem-filled life. Seeking Him with my whole heart might've had an effect on my circumstances, and decisions. Things might not have changed quickly. It took time for me to get myself into the mess I was in, and it would've certainly taken time to reverse those effects. It might, however, have encouraged me to view my current circumstances with hope instead of dread, affecting the decisions I made. The same is true for you as well. Whatever obstacle you're currently facing will eventually pass. Take the time to learn what you need to learn in that circumstance, and then move on and keep moving forward. If you focus your attention on what you've faced in the past, how you've been wronged or spend your time thinking about what you might be missing, you may fail to see what's before you and miss out on the really fulfilling, worth-while and cool plans God has for you.

As I stated in the beginning of this book, time keeps moving and it stops for no one, no matter who you are. Just as time moves, circumstances change. Don't get stuck in the mindset that life stinks and that it'll never change. That is an outright lie that Satan will plant in your mind to keep you chained down, if you refuse to fight it. Only you have the power to make the decision to do something to help yourself. Seek God with all your heart and your mind and you will find that freedom you so desire. He pursues you, why don't you try to seek Him?

In James chapter 1 it says that Word of God has the power to save our souls and set us free from the power of sin and death. If we want to escape the strongholds of bad habits in our lives we must be willing to grab a hold of our life preserver, which is the Bible. We must be deliberately reading God's Word, training our minds to be in tune with God so that we can experience the freedom that comes with obedience to it.

> *For if you listen to the word* (the Bible) *and don't obey it is like glancing at your face in a mirror. You see yourself, walk away, and forget what you look like. But if you look carefully into the perfect law that sets you free,* (the Bible) *and if you do what it says and don't forget what you heard, then God will bless you for doing it (James 1:23-25, NLT).*

As I've already stated the purpose of writing this book is to not only share the story of grace God has shown in my life that has revealed to me what true freedom is but also to inspire you to seek God yourself. An important question I'm going to ask you to think about two things. First, how badly do you want freedom? Secondly, how much of God do you want to see in your life? You and I must remember that God will unleash Himself and His power in our lives only as much as we allow Him to.

> *The Lord says, 'At just the right time, I will respond to you . . . I will say to the prisoners, 'Come out in freedom,' and to those in darkness, 'Come into the light.' . . . For the LORD in his mercy will lead them; he will lead them beside cool waters*
> (Isaiah 49:8-10, NLT).

I would like to encourage any person who is lost, is struggling in sin, or who is caught in the web of deceit to give up the fight, give in and embrace your need for God. God is there and He is just waiting for you, but He wants to connect with you personally, in your heart. The only thing left to ask is: *what are you waiting for?* Life is here and gone in an instant. Don't let yours go by and miss the purpose God has created you for, to know Him. If you don't know the Lord personally and you want to find the freedom that is in Christ, I want to give you the opportunity to enter into a personal relationship with Him. I have the prayer of salvation following this chapter.

Romans Road to Salvation

. . . for all have sinned and fall short of the glory of God . . . (Romans 3:23, NIV).

For the wages of sin is death, but the gift of God is eternal life in Christ Jesus our Lord (Romans 6:23, NIV).

But God demonstrates his own love for us in this: While we were still sinners, Christ died for us (Romans 5:8, NIV).

Everyone who calls on the name of the Lord will be saved (Romans 10:13, NIV).

That if you confess with your mouth, "Jesus is Lord," and believe in your heart that God raised him from the dead, you will be saved. For it is with your heart that you believe and are justified, and it is with your mouth that you confess and are saved (Romans 10:9-10, NIV).

Sinner's prayer of repentance:

God please forgive me for my sins. I am a sinner in need of a Savior. I do believe that Jesus died for my sins and He rose again three days later to conquer death, on my behalf. Thank you for saving me. I put my trust in YOU. In Jesus name I pray these things. Amen.

Thinking Question:

Do you know Jesus personally? If you just said the prayer above and you meant it, you do now! The next step is to get into a Bible believing church where you can talk to a pastor about being baptized and find out how to start your new life in Christ. If you didn't say that prayer but you felt the nudge don't put it off. Reach out to Him while you can.

Psalm 116:1-6, NLT

I love the Lord because he hears my voice
and my prayer for mercy.
Because he bends down to listen,
I will pray as long as I have breath!
Death wrapped its ropes around me;
the terrors of the grave overtook me.
I saw only trouble and sorrow.
Then I called on the name of the Lord:
"Please, Lord, save me!"
How kind the Lord is! How good he is!
So merciful, this God of ours!
The Lord protects those of childlike faith;
I was facing death, and he saved me.